Romans

Philip Steele

KINGFISHER

First published 2012 by Kingfisher
an imprint of Macmillan Children's Books
a division of Macmillan Publishers Limited
20 New Wharf Road, London N1 9RR
Basingstoke and Oxford
Associated companies throughout the world
www.panmacmillan.com

Series editor: Heather Morris
Literacy consultant: Hilary Horton

ISBN: 978-0-7534-3060-6
Copyright © Macmillan Publishers Ltd 2012

9 8 7 6 5 4 3 2 1

1TR/1011/WKT/UNTD/105MA

A CIP catalogue record for this book is available from
the British Library.

Printed in China

Picture credits
The Publisher would like to thank the following for permission to reproduce their images
(t = top, b = bottom, c = centre, r = right, l = left): Pages 4 Shutterstock/G2019; 5 Getty/Pierre Andrieu/AFP;
7b Corbis/Roger Ressmeyer; 10b Shutterstock/Sergielev; 11 Shutterstock/riekephotos; 13t Art Archive/
Archaeological Museum Alexandria/Dagli Orti; 15 Corbis/Massimo Borchi; 21t Art Archive/Musee de la
Civilisation Gallo-Romaine Lyon/Gianni Dagli Orti; 25 Shutterstock/Rui Vale de Sousa; 27 Art Archive/ Musee
Archaeologique Naples/Alfredo Dagli Orti; 28 Getty/Joseph Barrak/AFP; all other images Kingfisher artbank.

Contents

Roman treasure

The Romans ruled most of Europe more than 1,600 years ago. They also ruled many other lands. They came from a big city called Rome, in Italy.

Today we can still find things which the Romans made or used. People find the remains of Roman walls and buildings. They sometimes dig up old coins, pottery jars or rings and **brooches**. These help us to understand how the Romans lived.

Pont du Gard in France

A man scrapes away earth in a town called Bordeaux, in France. Underneath he finds a beautiful floor. It dates back to Roman times.

Finding out

In Italy there is a volcano called Vesuvius. It **erupted** in 79CE. There was a big explosion, which buried the town of Pompeii under ash and stones. Many people died.

Vesuvius erupting

Hundreds of years later, people cleared away the earth and rock. They could see the Roman houses and streets. There were shops, gardens, markets and theatres. People found pots and pans, and even left-over food. There were fine statues, musical instruments, jewellery and coins.

The barking dog

At the entrance to one house there was a picture of a fierce dog on a chain. Underneath were words meaning 'Beware of the dog'.

CAVE CANEM

Everyone could see for themselves how the Romans used to live. Here are the ruins of Pompeii today.

Rome and its empire

More than 2,700 years ago Rome was
just a few villages, built on hills near the
River Tiber. The villages joined up to
make a town, then the town became
a city. This city grew until Rome was
the biggest city in the world. About
a million people lived there.

The Romans sent armies to **conquer** other
lands. Spain, France, Britain and parts of
Germany were all ruled by the Romans.

The Romans ruled Romania, Greece, western Asia and North Africa too. These countries made up the Roman **empire**.

The wolf and the twins

An old **myth** said that twin baby boys called Romulus and Remus were left by the River Tiber. A wolf looked after them. When Romulus grew up, he became the first king of Rome.

The Romans built roads all over the empire.

Buying and selling

The Romans were great traders. They used coins made of gold, silver, bronze and copper. At Roman ports, ships were loaded with pottery and cloth. There were sacks of grain and jars of wine or olive oil. Traders argued over prices.

This Roman jar held wine or oil.

Roman coins

The Romans bought and sold people, too. They owned **slaves**. These people had no freedom and had to work hard for no money.

Pirate attack!
In 68BCE pirates attacked the Roman **port** of Ostia. The Romans built 500 ships to fight them. They captured many pirates.

Every Roman city had a place called the **forum**. People met here to do business. Around it were markets and shops.

Soldiers and war

The Roman army was divided into groups called **legions**. Each legion had its own badge, an eagle made of gold. Most soldiers fought on foot, but some fought on horseback.

Roman soldiers wore tunics and sandals or boots. They wore helmets and armour, and carried shields. Their weapons were short swords, daggers and spears.

A Roman soldier

One of the best Roman **generals** was called Julius Caesar. He won many battles for Rome. He became very powerful and so people were jealous of him. He was murdered in Rome in 44BCE.

Julius Caesar

The tortoise
Groups of Roman soldiers sometimes marched close together. They covered their heads and bodies with shields. They looked a bit like a tortoise, protected by a shell.

Gods and temples

The Romans believed in many different gods. Jupiter was the most important one. He was god of the sky. People believed that if they were bad, Jupiter might throw a **thunderbolt** at them. Other gods looked after different areas of life, such as war or love or the sea.

Jupiter

Juno

Diana

Mars

Neptune

Apollo

Venus

A temple in France

The Romans built temples for their gods and held festivals. The festival of Saturn was in the winter. People lit candles, had big feasts and gave presents.

A monster dog
Roman myths are full of monsters. Cerberus was a dog with three heads. He stopped dead people escaping into the world of the living.

At home

Romans believed that their homes were protected by gods and **spirits**. They made **offerings** to them every day.

There were many sorts of houses. In the biggest cities, such as Rome or Ostia, there were blocks of flats. Many towns had family houses with an open courtyard and pools of water. The roofs were made of tiles and the small windows had shutters.

In the country, rich people owned big houses called **villas**. Some had fine wall paintings, or floors decorated with **mosaics**. These were pictures made from small coloured stones or tiles.

This grand Roman house had lots of rooms, a garden and a courtyard.

Food and feasts

In the kitchen, slaves carried water and firewood. Pots and pans boiled on the brick stove. Cooks used olive oil, herbs and spices. A main dish might be pork, fish or chicken. There were onions, peas and cabbages, as well as figs and grapes. The Romans used honey to sweeten their food and drinks.

People did not eat much for breakfast or lunch. The main meal of the day was dinner. Some rich people held **banquets** where everyone ate too much. Guests lay on couches and ate from a low table, using their fingers and knives.

Feeling hungry?
Guests at a banquet might eat mice cooked in honey, snails in wine, dumplings made with brains, or even boiled ostrich.

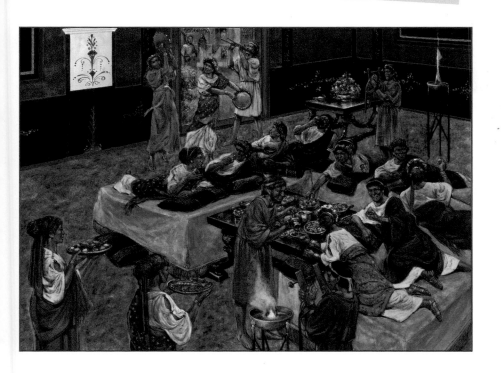

Getting dressed

A Roman lady might spend a long time getting ready in the morning. She put on a long tunic and then a woollen dress called a **stola** on top. She used perfume and jars of make-up, curled her hair and piled it up in the latest hairstyle. She tried on earrings and necklaces, then looked at herself in a mirror made of polished metal.

Pretty poison
Roman ladies liked to look pale. They made up their faces with chalk or white lead. The lead was poisonous and could make them ill.

Emerald
and gold
earrings

Children, slaves
and working people
all wore short tunics.
Important men wore
a heavy white robe
called a **toga**. They
wrapped it around
themselves and then
over one shoulder.

Thrills and spills

The Romans loved watching **chariot** races at a big track in Rome called the Circus Maximus. These were fast and very exciting. Sometimes the chariots crashed.

Roman charioteers

Romans also went to a big stadium called the Colosseum. Here they watched slaves and gladiators battle with each other until one was dead.

Every city had an open-air
theatre. The seats were
made of stone and arranged
in a semi-circle around the stage. The
actors wore masks. Most Romans liked
funny plays, but there were sad plays too.

Going to the baths

Every Roman town had public baths for men and women. Romans went there every day to meet their friends and relax. They often started with some exercises or games. Then they would try the pools, the hot tubs, the cold tubs and steam rooms. They might have a **massage**.

The Romans built bath houses at country villas and army forts. We can see Roman baths today at a city called Bath, in England.

The Roman baths in Bath

Cleaning up
Romans did not wash themselves with soap. They rubbed their bodies with oil and then scraped them clean.

Roman children

Roman babies played with clay rattles in the shape of animals. Toddlers played with marbles and dolls.

At about seven years old, some boys and girls learned reading, writing and arithmetic. They practised writing the alphabet. They used a sharp point to scrape the letters on boards covered in wax. If they made a mistake, they smoothed over the wax and started again.

Lucky charms

When children were born, they were given a charm called a bulla. The charm was to keep them safe. Girls wore the charm until they married. Boys wore theirs until they were 16.

Some boys from rich families went on to learn about history, poetry and making speeches. Some girls learned how to run a home, how to sew, and how to play a musical instrument with strings, called the cithara.

What happened to Rome?

The Romans fought their enemies for hundreds of years. It was difficult to rule such a large empire. Warriors attacked the forts along the borders and some even attacked Rome. The city became less powerful and other people became kings.

Many of the things we do today started in ancient Rome. The languages we speak, our laws, our buildings, even our cooking would not be the same without Rome.

A worker uncovers the ruins of a Roman bath house.

ROMAN DATES

BCE

753   Rome begins.

250   The Romans rule most of Italy.

58-50 Julius Caesar conquers Gaul
       (including modern-day France).

55-54 Julius Caesar attacks Britain.

44   Julius Caesar is murdered in Rome.

27   Rome is ruled by emperors.

CE

43   The Romans start to conquer Britain.

79   The volcano Vesuvius erupts in Italy.

117   The Roman empire is bigger than
       ever before.

330   Constantinople becomes capital
       of the Roman empire in the east.

410   Goths attack and capture Rome.

476   The Roman empire in the west comes
       to an end.

Glossary

banquet A big feast with invited guests.

brooch A piece of jewellery with a pin, used to decorate or fasten clothing.

chariot A light, fast carriage pulled by horses.

conquer To beat an enemy.

empire Lots of lands ruled by a single ruler or nation.

erupt To explode like a volcano.

forum The business centre and meeting place in an ancient Roman town.

general A senior army officer.

legion A large battle unit in the Roman army.

massage Rubbing muscles to help relax the body.

mosaic A picture made up of small pieces of coloured pottery, stone or glass.

myth An old story about gods, goddesses, heroes or monsters.

offering Something given to honour or please a god.

port A town by the sea, or on a lake or river, where ships can anchor.

slave Someone who is not free, and is forced to work for no money.

spirit A magical being bringing good or bad luck.

stola A long pleated dress worn over a tunic.

thunderbolt A lightning flash and a roll of thunder.

toga A white robe worn by important men in Rome.

villa A large Roman house.

Index